2014 Heritage Subdivision Real Estate Guide

2014 Heritage Subdivision Real Estate Guide
Copyright: Chandler Crouch Realtors
Published: 31st December 2013
ISBN: 978-1495451171
Publisher: Chandler Crouch Realtors

1st Edition
Please provide feedback and suggestions for us to consider for the 2nd Edition.
live@chandlercrouch.com

Table of Contents

About the Area

Alliance

While the Heritage subdivision is technically in Fort Worth, most residents identify with the newly built Alliance area and with close-by Keller. The Alliance area began to be thought of in 1985 when the Federal Aviation Administration (FAA) began seeking a location for a relief airport for DFW. The expansive acreage that would be needed forced the FAA to look to private landholders instead of cities. FAA approached the Perot family due to the large amount of land they had acquired in Tarrant and Denton counties and because of the family's reputation for providing acreage for public ventures.

The project continued to grow as key industry leaders advised that a reliever airport was too small and an industrial airport was brought up. This is when Ross Perot, Jr. began to envision an industrial development with an airport as an anchor that would spur the regional growth and attract other leading corporations to continue the cycle.

The name "Alliance" refers to the corroboration between the FAA, the City of Fort Worth and Hillwood. Hillwood is the company run by Ross Perot, Jr. and is the developer/planner for the Heritage subdivision and the Alliance Town Center.

The Fort Worth Alliance Airport opened on December 14, 1989 and became the world's first industrial airport. The addition of the BNSF Railway's Alliance Intermodal Facility in 1992 allowed Alliance to become a model for inland ports with abundant acreage surrounding direct access to air, rail, intermodal, and highway transportation options.

Keller

Originally, Keller was called Athol. Settlers began moving to Athol when rumors began to spread in 1879 that the Texas and Pacific Railway was coming to the northern part of the county. As the settlers hoped for the railway to make them a permanent stop, they agreed to change the name of the town to Keller after being urged to do so by the Texas Pacific foreman, John C. Keller. The train first came through in 1881. Keller is no longer served by the railroad, but rail traffic is still frequent as Texas and Pacific Railroad (now Union Pacific) still continues to use the tracks daily.

The Keller Independent School District serves more than 30,000 students and covers portions of Colleyville, Fort Worth, Haltom City, Hurst, North Richland Hills, Southlake, Watauga, Westlake and the entire city of Keller. Its tax rate is one of the lowest school tax rates in the county and enrollment in the district has doubled during the past ten years and expectations show to repeat the feat within the next decade. It is the ninth-fastest growing school district in Texas.

Money Magazine rated Keller as number 7 out of a 100 of the "Best Places to Live" in the United States for 2009 and American Community Survey listed Keller as number 59 of the Nation's Richest Cities with a median household income of $114,542. Southlake, a close neighbor, was ranked number 1. In the Best Places to Live it was also ranked number 4 for best city for Thanksgiving and number 4 for best city to relocate to in America.

Since 2000, Keller has had a population growth of 51%. The median home cost in Keller is $253,800 and homes appreciated in 2012 0.87percent. 81.09% of homes are owned, 15.09% are rented and only 3.82% are vacant.

The water quality is rated 90 out of 100 and the sales tax is 8.25%. The property tax rate is $.44219 per $100 in Keller which means that the owner of a $200,000 home pay approximately $885 a year in City property taxes. On average, the city has 36 inches of rain each and only .9 inches of snow. The city sees 67 precipitation days on average in a year which means plenty of sunshine for everyone. The average high in July is 96 degrees.

On a scale of 1 to 10 where 1 is low crime, Keller was rated a 1 for violent crime. The U.S. average is 4. On a scale of 1 to 10 where 1 is low crime, Keller was rated a 1 for property crime. The U.S. average is 4.

Dallas/Fort Worth

The latest U.S. census data revealed that Fort Worth grew by 38.6 percent since 2000, adding over 200,000 new residents, with much of that growth taking place in the north Fort Worth corridor around Alliance. Fort Worth was ranked as the fastest-growing large city (population over 500,000) in the entire U.S. for the past decade, and Tarrant County grew by over 25 percent during the period, adding more than 350,000 residents. The current population of the Fort Worth is estimated to be about 778,000. The most recent estimate of population for the entire Dallas/Fort Worth metroplex comes in at 6,526,548 people.

According to a 2011 study by the Gadberry Group, an Arkansas-based intelligence service and data collection firm, the Haslet and north Fort Worth area surrounding Alliance was the second-fastest growing area in the nation, experience a 735 percent growth from 2000 to 2010. Keller ranked as the third-fastest growing community in the national study growing by more than 226 percent during the same period. Both areas brought more than 35,000 households to the Alliance region from 2000-2010.

According to the U.S. Government, the DFW metroplex includes the following counties: Collin, Dallas, Denton, Ellis, Hood, Hunt, Johnson, Kaufman, Parker, Rockwall, Tarrant and Wise counties.

Dallas/Fort Worth serves as the state's banking and financial center. It is also where the 5th busiest airport in the world resides, DFW. It is a major wholesale and distribution center by air and land. Additionally, high-tech industries such as telecommunications have contributed to the growth in the Metroplex.

Dallas landed in the top 10 on Forbes' list of "Best Bank for the buck cities". All 4 Texaplex cities were in Forbes top 10 "Best Cities to Buy a Home" as well.

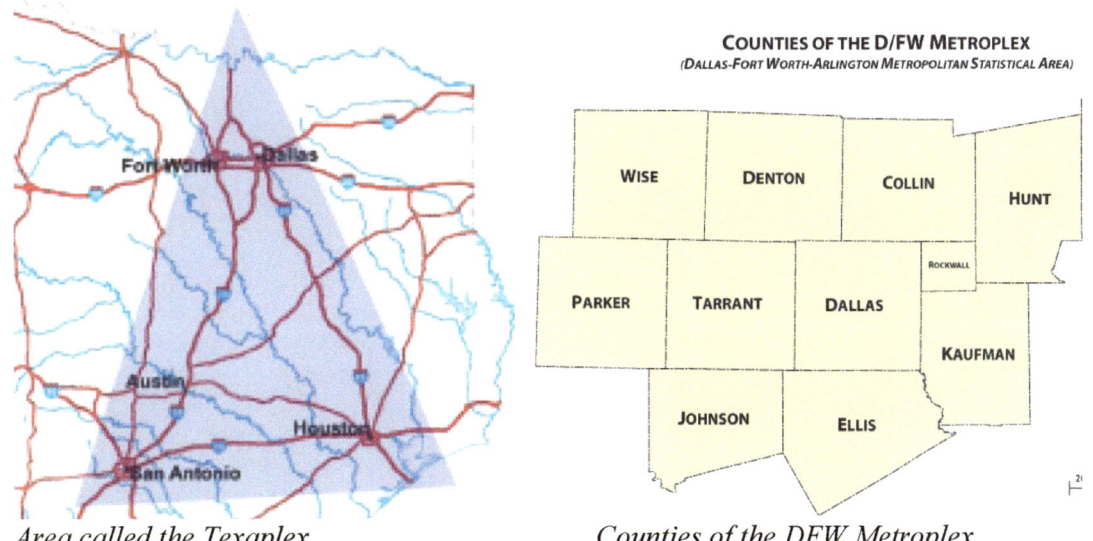

Area called the Texaplex   *Counties of the DFW Metroplex*

Texas

USA Today reported in a July 25, 2011 article that "Texas' population grew by 4.3 million, or 21%, during the past decade, more than twice the national pace. About half the total was because of births, but Texas also gained 849,000 residents via state-to-state migration, second only to Florida." The increase in the Texas population is not a new occurrence. According to the Dallas Federal Reserve, Texas has outpaced the nation's growth since the early 1900's.

Approximately 80 percent of Texas residents live in what is known as the Texaplex. This is the triangular region made up of Dallas/Fort Worth, Houston, San Antonio and Austin. Due to Texas' economic conditions, geographical location, natural resources, infrastructure, political conditions and even weather has created a perfect storm of opportunity and growth that is greatly outpacing the rest of the nation. Even in a time of a national recession Texas holds strong and stable and is the fastest growing state in the nation. More Fortune 500 companies call Texas home than any other state.

Texas has approximately 26 million people living it. If it were its own country, it would be the 10th largest in the world. It would have the 12th largest economy, based on gross domestic product, ahead of Mexico, Russia and India. It would be the 5th largest oil and gas producing country in the world.

Texas is big and is getting bigger. More than 1,000 people a day move to Texas. Texas dominated the list of the nation's fastest growing cities with San Antonio, Fort Worth, Houston, Austin and Dallas all landing in the Top 10.

CNBC named Texas the #1 state for doing business. In 2007, half of all jobs created in the US were in Texas. There is no income tax, no tax on goods in transit and its location in the central time zone makes it ideal for working with companies on either coast.

Texas has teams represented in all of the major professional sports: football, baseball, hockey, basketball, and soccer. The Texas Rangers (baseball) and Dallas Cowboys (football) call Arlington their home.

A Look into the Villages of Heritage

The Bluffs

These homes are built by Standard Pacific and start at $370,000. It is one of two of the last villages you are able to buy new homes in Heritage. Standard Pacific has been building homes since 1965. They have built homes in Shady Oaks, Southlake; Turnberry at Trophy Club; Winding Creek, Southlake; Carlisle at Lantana and Laviana at Lantana in Texas.

The Bluffs was voted Community of the Year by the Dallas Builders Association. You can choose between 13 unique home plans ranging from 2586 to 4353 square feet, 3 to 6 bedrooms, and 2.5 to 5.5 bathrooms. All homes are fenced, have large kitchens, energy-efficient items, inside the gated community, and have already been sodded and landscaped when you move in!

Personalization includes 6 cabinet types, 6 countertop types, 5 backsplash types, 6 flooring types. Options include flexible room conversions, built in cabinetry, spa-like bathroom fixtures, tubs and features, designer kitchen cabinetry, gourmet ranges and features, granite countertops, high performance appliances, energy efficiency and ecofriendly products, upgraded hardwood and tile flooring, and premium carpet

The Bluffs Village Home

Interior of a Bluffs Village Home

The Bluffs Village Home

Interior of a Bluffs Village Home

Designs Available in The Bluffs Ready to Build

- The **Weatherford** starts at $373,000. It has 2710 square feet and 4 bedrooms. You can choose to have 3 or 3.5 bathrooms built.
- The **Buchanan** starts at $380,000. It has 2913 square feet and 4 bedrooms. You can choose to have 3 or 3.5 bathrooms built.
- The **Granbury** starts at $394,000. It has 3171 square feet and a choice of 3 or 4 bedrooms. You can build 2.5 to 3.5 bathrooms
- The **Monticello** starts at $401,000. It has 3217 square feet and 4 bedrooms. You can have 3 to 4 bathrooms built.
- The **Rainier** starts at $395,000. It has 3291 square feet and a choice of 4 or 5 bedrooms. You can choose to have 3 to 4 bathrooms built.
- The **Sweetwater** starts at $401,000. It has 3478 square feet and a choice of 4 or 5 bedrooms. You can choose to have 3.5 to 4.5 bathrooms built.
- The **Kensington** starts at $414,000. It has 3603 square feet and a choice of 4 or 5 bedrooms. You can build 3 to 4.5 bathrooms.
- The **Glen Rose** starts at $406,000. It has 3621 square feet and a choice of 4, 5 or 6 bedrooms. You can choose to have 4 to 6 bathrooms built.
- The **Benbrook** starts at $413,000. It has 3672 square feet and a choice of 4 or 5 bedrooms. You can have 3.5 to 4.5 bathrooms built.
- The **Travis** starts at $424,000. It has 3823 square feet and a choice of 4 or 5 bedrooms. You can have 4.5 to 5.5 bathrooms built.
- The **Lantana** starts at $415,000. It has 3856 square feet and a choice of 4 or 5 bedrooms. You can have 3.5 to 5 bathrooms built.
- The **Marshalla** starts at $448,000. It has 3979 square feet and a choice of 4 or 5 bedrooms. You can have 4.5 to 5 bathrooms built.
- The **Remington** starts at $427,000. It has 4192 square feet, 5 bedrooms and 4 bathrooms.

Please discuss with your realtor the designs you are interested in for more information, photos and layouts.

Elm Fork – David Weekly

Homes located in the Elm Fork portion of the Heritage subdivision are built by David Weekly Homes or by Highland Homes. Both types of homes offer a three level warranty. The first level is a 1 year limited warranty plus the appliance manufacturer's warranties. Level 2 is the mechanical systems warranty that covers plumbing, electrical, central air conditioning and heating systems. Level 3 covers any major structural defects during the first 10 years. This village is the second to last one available for new homes.

Elm Fork Village Home

Elm Fork Village Home

Elm Fork Village Home

David Weekly has 9 different types of designs available currently.

David Weekly Homes Available

- **The Begonia** starts at $267,000. It has 1910 square feet and can be one or two stories. It can have 3 to 5 bedrooms and 2 to 3.5 bathrooms. You also have the option for a 2 or 3 car garage.
- **The Savino** starts at $282,000. It has 2140 square feet and is one story. It can have 2 or 3 bedrooms, 2.5 bathrooms and a 2 car garage.
- **The Kale** starts at $290,000. It has 2353 square feet and is one story. It can have 4 or 5 bedrooms and 3 to 4.5 bathrooms. The garage can be 2 or 3 cars.
- **The Larmona** starts at $293,000. It has 2425 square feet and is one story. It can have 3 or 4 bedrooms with 2 to 3 bathrooms and a 2 car garage.
- **The Cruise** starts from $305,000. It can have 2734 to 2794 square feet and is 2 stories. It has 4 bedrooms, 3.5 bathrooms and a 2 car garage.
- **The Martelle** starts at $307,000. It has 2913 square feet and is two stories. It can have 3 to 5 bedrooms and 2.5 to 4.5 bathrooms. It comes with a 3 car garage.
- **The Michaelson** starts at $316,000. It can have 3293 to 3350 square feet and is two stories. It has 5 bedrooms, 4 bathrooms and a 2 car garage.
- **The Jewell** starts at $318,000. It has 2692 square feet and is two stories. It can have 4 to 5 bedrooms. It comes with 3 bathrooms and a 2 car garage.
- **The Weidman** starts at $321,000. It can have 3174 to 3213 square feet and is two stories. It can have 5 to 6 bedrooms. It comes with 4.5 bathrooms and a 2 car garage.

Please discuss with your realtor the designs you are interested in for more information, photos and layouts.

Elm Fork – Highland Homes

Highland Homes has 12 floor plans available. Optional features include: an extended master bedroom, an extended family room, an upgraded master bathroom, additional bathrooms, additional bedrooms or studios, additional game rooms, bookshelves and more.

Elm Fork Village Home

Elm Fork Village Home

Highland Homes Available

- **518T** starts at $283,000. It has 2010 square feet and comes with 3 bedrooms, 2 bathrooms, 2 car garage and is one story. There is a new home that has had construction completed on the market that has had its price dropped to $275,000
- **512T** starts at $286,000. It has 2236 square feet, 3 bedrooms, 2 bathrooms, 2 car garage and is one story.
- **511T** starts at $287,000. It has 2198 square feet, 3 bedrooms, 2. 5 bathrooms, 2 car garage and is one story.
- **502** starts at $303,000. It has 2372 square feet, 3 bedrooms, 2.5 bathrooms, 2 car garage and is one story.
- **538** starts at $303,000. It has 2253 square feet, 3 bedrooms, 2.5 bathrooms, 2 car garage and is one story.
- **529** starts at $306,000. It has 2492 square feet, 4 bedrooms, 2.5 bathrooms, 2 car garage and is 2 stories.
- **533** starts at $314,000. It has 2697 square feet, 3 bedrooms, 2.5 bathrooms, 2 car garage and is 2 stories
- **513** starts at $318,000. It has 2733 square feet, 3 bedrooms, 2.5 bathrooms, 2 car garage and is two stories.
- **514** starts at $324,000. It has 3130 square feet, 4 bedrooms, 2.5 bathrooms, 2 car garage, and is two stories.
- **527** starts at $329,000. This is the model home plan (the model home shows some options available). It has 3202 square feet, 4 bedrooms, 2.5 bathrooms, 2 car garage and is two stories.
- **535** starts at $332,000. It has 2973 square feet, 4 bedrooms, 3 bathrooms, 2 car garage and is two stories.
- **537** starts at $336,000. It has 3058 square feet, 4 bedrooms, 3 bathrooms, 2 car garage and is two stories.

Please discuss with your realtor the designs you are interested in for more information, photos and layouts.

West Fork

D.R. Horton was the primary builder in the West Fork village. No new homes are available, but pre-owned homes are available. D.R. Horton is the largest residential house builder in the United States at the end of September in 2012. It was originally founded in 1978 by Donald R. Horton and has its headquarters in the D.R. Horton Tower in Downtown Fort Worth.

They only build single-detached homes, but they are in 71 markets and 26 states. Homes in West Fork range from 1300 square feet to 3750 square feet. Bedrooms range from 3 to 5, bathrooms from 2 to 4, and the home can be 1 or 2 stories. There are also many 2 and 3 car garages to choose from.

West Fork Village Home

West Fork Village Home

Winfield

Winfield includes homes built by both Highland Homes and Standard Pacific. No new homes are available, but pre-owned homes range from 1800 square feet to 4500 square feet. They have 3 to 5 bedrooms, 2 to 4 bathrooms, and 2 to 3 garage spaces.

Winfield was the first village to be built and was started in 2001 and was finished in 2005. Most homes were built in 2001 and 2002.

Winfield Village Home

Winfield Village Home

Trinity

The Trinity village was built by Standard Pacific homes. This village was built from 2003 to 2008 with the majority of homes being built between 2004 and 2006. These homes range from 3 bedrooms to 6 bedrooms and anywhere from 2 bathrooms to 4. 2 or 3 car garages are common and the homes can range in size from 1800 square feet to 3500 square feet.

This section extends from Bayard Street west to North Beach St and Shiver Rd north to Heritage Trace Pkwy.

Trinity Village Home

Trinity Village Home

Cape Cod

      Cape Cod is a separate part of the Trinity Village that stretches from Heritage Trace Pkwy south to Shiver Rd and from Haas Dr and McCauleys Dr east to Ray White Rd. It is referred to by this name as most of the homes in this area have the Cape Cod cottage style.

      A Cape Cod cottage is a style of house originating in New England in the 17th century. It is characterized by a low, broad frame building, generally a story and a half high, with a steep pitched roof and very little ornamentation. Homes were designed to withstand the stormy, stark weather of the Massachusetts coast.

      Homes in this section are typically one and half stories with an extra living room or other room located upstairs. D.R. Horton started construction in 2004 and continued through 2010. The bulk of the homes were built in 2004 and 2005. Homes have either 3 or 4 bedrooms and 2 to 2.5 bathrooms. They can range from 1500 square feet to 2800 square feet.

Cape Cod Village Home

Cape Cod Village Home

Moncrief

Again, Standard Pacific homes had a hand in building this village in Heritage. Many of the homes in this village are larger with at least 4 bedrooms and 2.5 bathrooms. They can have up to 6 bedrooms and 4 bathrooms. This was one of the first villages built as many homes were built in 2003, but construction continued until 2007. The size of the homes range from 2600 square feet to 4400 square feet with two or three garage spaces included. This village has one of the lowest turnover rates in the subdivision.

Moncrief Village Home

Moncrief Village Home

Clear Fork

Highland Homes was one of the main builders in the Clear Fork subdivision. Due to Sinclair St connecting both villages of Clear Fork and Elm Fork, the two villages are very similar and relate to each other. Most of the homes in Clear Fork have 3 bedrooms, but can have up to 5. They have 2 to 3.5 bathrooms and all have 2 car garages.

They can range in size from 1800 square feet up to 3100 square feet. This is one of the later built subdivisions as most of the homes were not built until 2006-2007. Construction did start in 2004 and was completed in 2007.

Clear Fork Village Home

Clear Fork Village Home

Heritage HOA

The Heritage subdivision has been approved for a Public Improvement District Number 7 - a special taxing district. As such, the city of Fort Worth uses special tax dollars to enhance and maintain area parks, entryways, rights-of-way, fencing, irrigation systems etc. in a manner that exceeds the standard services provided by the city of Fort Worth. This means that residents living within the boundaries of the PID will pay an extra tax in the amount of $.21 per $100 of the assessed value.

Why are there still HOA dues for homes in the area? This is due to the fact that the PID cannot pay for any maintenance that is not benefiting the public at large. This means that the extra money given to the PID cannot help maintain the Clubhouse, swimming pools or sports courts. The HOA dues help to fill in the gap to keep the community beautiful and vibrant with activities for the entire family and friends.

Some of the amenities that the HOA provides include fitness center at The Clubhouse, Great Room and indoor kitchen at The Clubhouse (TC), WiFi Service at The Clubhouse, covered patio with seating and outdoor grill at TC, 10 acre aquatic complex with lagoon pool, waterfall, waterslides, lap pool, kiddie pools, splash bucket pool and cabanas, parks and playgrounds, open spaces and green belts on the 200 acres of the neighborhood, hiking and biking trails, and a 7500 foot recreational center.

Currently, membership dues are $385 a year and are collected semi-annually. An initiation fee of $200 is due upon closing a home in Heritage. Premier Communities manages the HOA and the primary contact for Heritage is Kyle Clawson. He can be reached at heritagemanager@premiercommunities.net or (817) 741-1912. He is at 3102 Oak Lawn Ave Ste 202 Dallas, TX 75219

Schools

General

The Heritage community has three elementary schools, six intermediate/middle school and two high schools that serve the community. All of them are highly rated and have been recognized in various aspects. Here is the most up to date information available on various aspects of the community!

The district has been in place since 1911, but has only see a large amount of growth in the past three decades. It is now one of the largest districts in the Dallas/Fort Worth metroplex. Some of their recent awards include two National Blue Ribbon Schools of Excellence, 26 TEA Exemplary and Recognized schools, the 2007 Texas State Secondary Teacher of the Year and the 2008 Texas State Elementary Teacher of the Year.

Every year, the district asks parents to fill out a survey with a list of questions about what the parents think of the job they are doing with their kids. For 2013, the results were positive, but also called for more career and technical training. Some other main interests were better communication with school district leadership and less focus and teaching investment on standardized testing. The survey is taken voluntarily online.

Most of the schools in the Keller ISD have adopted a Watch Dog program which encourages students' fathers to sign up and be at the school for a day. It helps students feel safer and allows the dads a behind the scenes look at the campus.

All schools in Keller ISD are using the Home Access Center which allows parents to see important information pertaining to their child(rens) including class schedules, emergency

contact information, attendance and grades. No report cards will be sent home with the students. Access can be gained by going to:
http://www.kellerisd.net/studentsandfamilies/know/Pages/HomeAccessCenter.aspx

Due to the nature of schools, the boundaries shown during the following sections may not be perfect. Please refer to http://www.kellerisd.net for the most up to date and accurate information

Awards

- KISD has earned a 5 star rating for Financial Efficiency for the third straight year.
- KISD received the Texas Honors Circle Awards for Public Education Excellence which awards them for having achieved academic success through cost-effective operations.
- Has received the Indoor Air Quality National Model of Sustained Excellence Award which is given to U.S. school districts that demonstrate ongoing exceptional commitment and achievement in maintaining healthy education facilities while institutionalizing comprehensive Indoor Air Quality (IAQ) management goals, and tracked short term and long term progress on IAQ management.
- 2010 Clean Air Award – National Air Filtration Association which is to recognize the efforts of facility managers and building owners who go above and beyond the recommended minimums and put into place best practice maintenance.
- TASA/TASB Architectural Award was given to Timber Creek High School for the design and construction of the school.
- More awards given to the district and individual schools can be found by going to: http://www.kellerisd.net/district/who/Pages/DistrictAccomplishments.aspx

Elementary Schools

Bette Perot Elementary (BPE)

In the Heritage subdivision, Bette Perot serves mainly West Fork, Winfield and Moncrief sections.

The school has a 96.3% attendance rate which is above the district goal of 96%. There are 705 students attending the school currently. Class sizes are typically between 17.4 and 19.3 children. The school has 56.3 total staff with 43.7 staff members being teachers.

3 teachers are brand new to teaching. 11.7 have 1-5 years of experience. 12.9 have 6-10 years of experience. 13 have 11-20 years and 3.1 have over 20 years of experience.

The average amount spent per student is $5,837.

Some fun facts about the school, is they provide a list of "teacher favorites" at the beginning of each year for you to get to know the individual teachers more.

They also have an emergency center located at Northwood Church in Keller if an emergency happens during school hours. This is where parents need to go and call for information to help clear traffic and phone lines for the emergency responders. It is located at 1870 Rufe Snow Dr in Keller and the phone number is 817-656-8150.

The school is currently raising $50,000 for a new playground they hope to begin building soon.

The school mascot is the Patriots and their colors are red, white and blue.

Lone Star Elementary

This elementary school serves the Trinity and Cape Cod areas which are near Central High school and the YMCA.

They have a 96.9% attendance rate which exceeds the district goal of 96%. They have a total of 727 students. The class sizes are usually 20 with the lowest being 18.9 in 1st grade and the highest having 21.3 students in kindergarten. The school has 54.8 total staff members with 43.4 members of the staff as teachers.

0.4 of those teachers have had no experience teaching. 17 have 1-5 years of experience. 11 have 6-10 years of experience. 12 have 11-20 years and 3 have over 20 years.

The average spent per student is $5324

Some fun facts about this school is they have moved to a full day for kindergarten to help with the continuing development of students.

The school mascot is The Lone Star Texan and their colors are red, white and blue.

Eagle Ridge Elementary

This elementary school serves all of Heritage north of Heritage Trace and west of N Beach in addition to the Clear Fork area.

The school has a 96.2% attendance rate which is above the district goal of 96%. It has 737 total students. Class sizes are around 21 with the lowest being 19.1 in 1st grade and the highest being 22 in 2nd grade. The school has 55.2 total staff with 43.8 of the staff members being teachers.

4.9 teachers are brand new. 15.3 have 1-5 years of experience. 11.9 have 6-10 years of experience. 11.6 have 11-20 years and none of the teachers have over 20 years of experience.

The average spent on each student is $5,779.

The school mascot is the Eagles and their school colors are blue and white.

Intermediate/Middle Schools

Trinity Meadows Intermediate

This intermediate school serves 5th and 6th graders in the Clear Fork, The Bluffs and areas north of Heritage Trace Parkway and east of N Beach St.

The school has a 96.2% attendance rate which is slightly above the 96% district goal. They have 960 total students. Class sizes are between 24.6 and 27.2 students. The school has 73.1 total staff with 53.3 being teachers.

0.8 out of the 53.3 teachers are brand new. 18 have 1-5 years of experience. 17.5 have 6-10 years of experience. 16 have 11-20 years of experience and 1 has 20 years of experience.

The average spent per student is $5,845.

The school mascot is the Mustang and their colors are red, black and white. They opened in the fall of 2006.

Trinity Springs Middle

This middle school serves 7th and 8th graders in the Clear Fork, The Bluffs, and areas north of Heritage Trace Parkway and east of N Beach St.

The school has a 96.1% attendance rate which is slightly above the 96% district goal. The school has 937 total students. The class size is between 19 and 24.6 students. They have 79.5 total staff with 58 of them as teachers.

1.8 of the teachers are brand new. 27.1 have 1-5 years of experience. 15.5 have 6-10 years of experience. 13.7 teachers have 11-20 years of experience and none have over 20 years of experience.

The average spent per student is $5,845.

The school mascot is the Titans and their colors are green and yellow.

Parkwood Hill Intermediate

This intermediate school serves 5th and 6th graders in the Trinity and Cape Cod areas.

The school has a 95.9% attendance rate which is just below the 96% district goal. It has 1173 total students with class sizes between 26.7 and 27.4 students. They have 81.5 total staff with 62.9 being teachers.

No teachers are brand new at the school, but 22.1 have 1-5 years of experience. 15.4 have 6-10 years of experience. 21.4 have 11-20 years and 4 have over 20 years of experience.

Average spent per student is $5,030.

The school mascot is the Bulldogs and their colors are purple and gold.

Hillwood Middle

This middle school serves 7th and 8th graders in the Trinity and Cape Cod areas.

It has a 96% attendance rate. It has 1180 total students with class sizes in between 19.3 and 26.8 students. They have 83.3 total staff with 65.9 being teachers.

The school has 3 brand new teachers. 29.5 teachers have 1-5 years of experience. 11.6 have 6-10 years. 18.9 have 11-20 years of experience and 2.8 have over 20 years.

The average spent per student is $5,338.

The school mascot is the Wolves and their colors are blue and gold.

Chisholm Trail Intermediate

This intermediate school serves 5th and 6th graders in West Fort, Elm Fork, Moncrief, and Winfield areas.

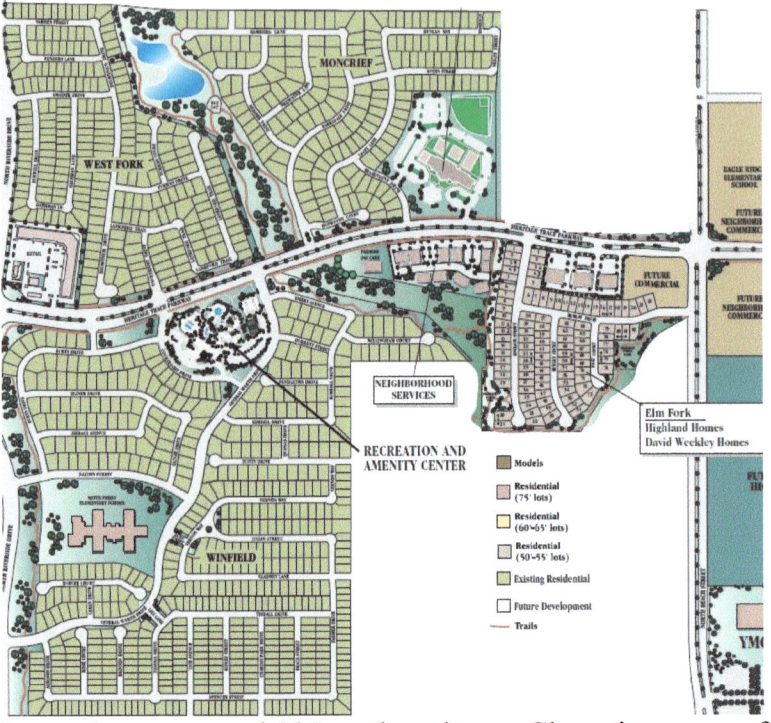

It has a 96% attendance rate and 895 total students. Class sizes range from 25.4 to 26.6. The total staff is 70.6 with 51.7 being teachers.

No teachers are brand new and 17.2 have 1-5 years of experience. 16.9 have 6-10 years of experience. 11.1 have 11-20 years of experience and 6.5 have over 20 years of experience.

The average cost per student is $5,482

The school mascot is the Pioneers and their colors are red and blue.

Fossil Hill Middle

This middle school serves 7th and 8th graders in West Fork, Elm Fork, Moncrief, and Winfield.

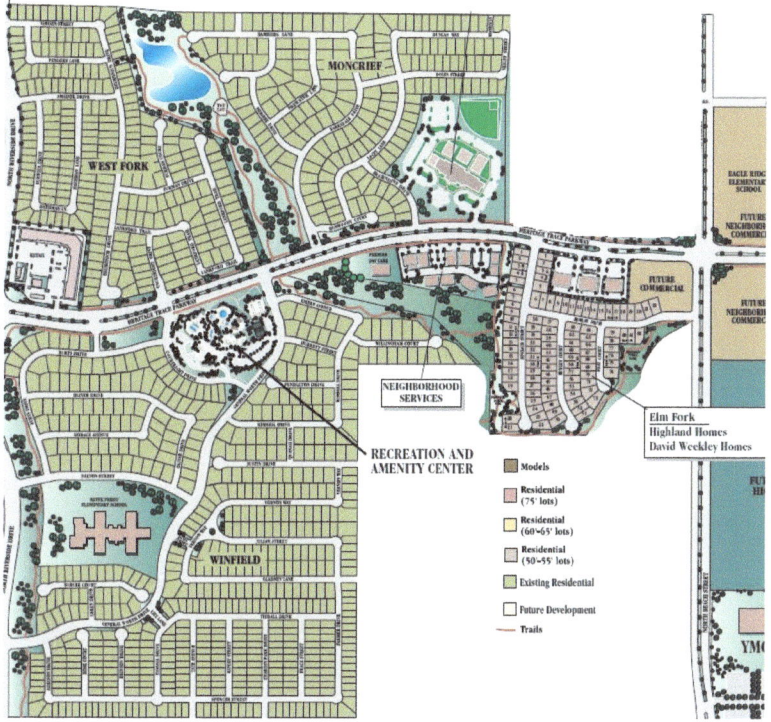

It has a 95.6% attendance rate and 888 total students. Class sizes range from 20.1 and 27.6 students. They have 74.7 total staff with 54.4 being teachers.

No teachers are brand new. 17.5 have 1-5 years of experience. 10.9 have 6-10 years of experience. 17.8 have 11-20 years of experience and 8.3 have over 20 years of experience.

The average cost per student is $6,071.

The school mascot is the Wildcats and their school colors are gold and black.

Timberview Middle

No attendance rate statistics are available at this time. The school serves fifth through eighth graders and is located on Old Denton Rd past Heritage Trace Pkwy.

It has a total of 953 students with class sizes between 31.2 and 32 students. They have a total of 68.7 staff with 53 of them being teachers.

9.6 teachers are brand new to teaching. 20 have 1-5 years of experience. 11.6 have 6-10 years of experience. 11.8 have had 16-20 years of experience and no teachers have over 20 years of experience.

The average cost per student is $5,838

This is a "guinea pig" school and was opened in 2011. It is highly technology based with IPad and Mac books located consistently throughout the school. While it had a rough start, the school has blossomed and continues to grow.

School boundaries can change, but currently homes in the northern part of Winfield and West Fork can go to Timberview.

The school mascot is the Hawks and their colors are purple and white.

Timber Creek High

This high school serves the students in Clear Fork, West Fork, Moncrief, and Winfield.

It has a 95.5% attendance rate which is the highest out of the three high schools in the area. It has a total of 1560 students and class sizes are between 16.9 and 25.3 students. They have 122.1 total staff with 95 of them being teachers.

15.9 teachers are brand new. 20.7 have 1-5 years of experience. 28.5 have 6-10 years of experience. 22 have 11-20 years of experience and 7.9 have over 20 years of experience.

The average spent per student is $7,675

The school mascot is the Falcon and their colors are purple and gold.

Central High

This high school serves the students in Trinity, The Bluffs and the homes north of Heritage Trace and east of North Beach.

It has a 94.3% attendance rate. It has 2618 total students and class sizes are between 20.9 and 25.4 students. They have 187.1 total staff with 139.5 being teachers.

4.3 teachers are brand new. 41.3 have 1-5 years of experience. 39.9 have 6-10 years of experience. 44.6 have 11-20 years of experience and 9.4 have over 20 years of experience.

The average spent per student is $6,001.

The school mascot is the Chargers and their colors are crimson and gold.

Shopping and Entertainment

Child-Friendly Activities
The Heritage HOA comes with many activities for kids including a 10 acre aquatic complex with lagoon pool, waterfall, waterslides, lap pool, kiddie pools, splash bucket pool and cabanas, parks and playgrounds, open spaces and green belts on the 200 acres of the neighborhood, hiking and biking trails, and a 7500 foot recreational center.

Libraries
There are several libraries near the subdivision, although the closet one is the Fort Worth – Summerglen branch located on 4205 Basswood Blvd Fort Worth, TX 76137. Other alternatives include the Keller Public Library on 640 Johnson Rd Keller, TX 76248 and the Watauga Public Library on 7109 Whitley Rd Fort Worth, TX 76148. You would only need the Fort Worth Public Library card to visit any of these locations.

Fort Worth - Summerglen Branch
The Summerglen library is open from 10 to 6 Monday through Wednesday, 12 to 8 on Thursday and 10 to 6 on Saturday. It is closed on Friday and Sunday. The library was opened on November 11th, 2000 and is 11,068 square feet.
Some of the special collections it has includes:
- middle school,
- teen,
- large print books,
- entertainment and instruction media,
- Games for all ages for use in library.

A special service this branch offers is preschool story time which is held at 10:30am on Mondays, 4 pm on Wednesdays and 7 pm on Thursdays. The library also offers Wii gaming, a fiction book group, a non-fiction book club, junior and adult volunteer programs and a meeting room rental.
For more information, go to http://fortworthtexas.gov/library/branches/Summerglen/

Keller Public Library
The Keller library is open Monday through Wednesday from 10 to 8, Thursday and Friday from 10 to 6, and Saturday and Sunday 12 to 5. It is open 7 days a week minus holidays. The library was expanded in 2010 after citizens of Keller approved a $4 million library bond on November 6, 2007. This turned the former 12,500 square foot facility into a 22,000 square foot facility which includes three meeting rooms, quiet reading areas, computers for children, teens and adults, and a covered patio. The renovation was completed on March 6, 2010.
One of the unique features this library offers is a drive through pickup window. You can search the Library Catalog from home and simply drive up to the window to check out the books. It is near the library's book drop on the west side of the building.
The library also has children's story times at:
Monday: 11am – Spanish Storytime
      6pm – Family Storytime
Tuesday: 10:15am – Preschool – agent 3-6

11am – Baby Time – up to 18 months
11:30am – Toddler 18-36 months
Wednesday: 10:15am – Preschool – agent 3-6
11am – Baby Time – up to 18 months
11:30am – Toddler 18-36 months
Saturday: 12:15pm – Preschool – agent 3-6
1pm – Baby Time – up to 18 months
1:30am – Toddler 18-36 months

The library goes a step further and has a Summer Reading Club to help children with prizes, performers and accountability to read when they off from school.
For even more information, go to http://www.cityofkeller.com/index.aspx?page=35

Watauga Public Library
The Watauga Public Library is open Monday and Thursday from 12 pm to 8 pm, Tuesday, Wednesday and Friday from 10 am to 6 pm and Saturday from 12 pm to 4 pm. They are closed on Sundays. The library opened in October of 1983, but was expanded in 2007 to make it 20,413 square feet which now includes two large and four small study rooms and a meeting room to provide quiet areas for study or meetings. One of the hallmark features of the library is a woodland mural painted by book illustrator Liz Bonham.

Story time occurs on Tuesday and Wednesday at 10 am. They also have a Summer Reading Club which is the largest in North Texas. They have approximately 2,000 children participate each year.

Shopping Centers and More

The Alliance Town Center on I-35W and Heritage Trace Pkwy has almost all of your shopping needs taken care of in a close and convenient location. Below is just a small portion of the shops currently located in the center:

- *Movie Theater:* Cinemark
- *Department Stores:* JCPenney

  Belk
- *Medical:* Fort Worth Pediatric Urgent Care

  The Joint…the chiropractic place
- *Grocery:* Kroger
- *Cleaning:* Cinch Cleaners
- *Health and Beauty:* Hand and Stone Massage and Facial Spa

  Massage Envy

  KoKo Fit Club

  Palm Beach Tan

  Sports Clips

  Great Clips

To see more stores and a list of dining experiences located in the Alliance Town Center please visit: http://www.alliancetowncenter.com/Directory.aspx

Other stores nearby include:

- Walmart (Beach and N Tarrant Pkwy)
- Home Depot (off of Hwy 377 and N Tarrant Pkwy)
- Michaels (off of Hwy 377 and N Tarrant Pkwy)

Future Development

Construction

I-35W Development

So far, $415 million has been provided to the city to expand sections of I-35W from I-30 up to Hwy 287/Decatur cut off. The goal is to add 4 toll lanes. Right now, the maximum initial travel cost is set at .75 cents per mile.

Segment 3A is north of I-30 to I-820 and is 6.7 miles. It is expected to be completed in 2018.

Segment 3B is from I-820 to Hwy 287/Decatur cut off. This section is approximately 3.5 miles and is expected to be completed in 2017.

Segments 3A and 3B have been funded and started.

Segment 3C is from Hwy 287/Decatur cut off to Eagle Parkway. This segment has been planned, but funding has not been identified yet.

Beach Street Construction

This project was approved by Fort Worth voters in the 2008 Capital Improvements Program which will turn Beach St between Vista Meadows Dr to south of Shiver Rd into a 4 lane divided arterial street with curbs, raised median, left and right turn lanes, storm drain system, streetlights, bike lanes, sidewalks, and 3 new traffic signals at the Alta Vista Rd, Heritage Trace Pkwy and Shiver Rd intersections. Michael Weiss is the project manager.

It was started in April 2013 and is estimated to be completed in April of 2015.

Beach St is expected to be open with one lane in each direction on November 22, 2013 which was delayed from November 15, 2013. The contractors have agreed to pay the city damages for up to $7,000 per day for every day the closure lasts beyond November 15th.

The closure was decided on because it allows the contractor to complete the overall construction 9 months earlier than planned. If the closure had not been done, the contractor would have had to remove about 25 feet of earth on half of the hill, open the lanes and then try to shave off the 25 feet of earth on the other half of the hill while people are driving underneath them.

The work is part of a long term plan to make N Beach St a viable north-south alternative to I-35W for local traffic – not trucks or other long distance travelers – over the next two decades. An estimated 36,000 vehicles per day travel N Beach just north of I-820.

Old Denton Rd/North Riverside Construction

This project started on June 10, 2013 and is expected to be completed in August of 2014. They are expanding the road to include four divided lanes with bike lanes on both sides. Phase 2 of this project just started in October 2013 and will last through March 2014. It is the largest portion of the project as they have to grade the hills and flatten. Utilities will be coming down and will be underground on the east side. A roundabout is going to be located at Crawford Farms Dr and N Riverside Dr.

The school zone speed is currently set at 30 miles per hour instead of the usual 20 miles which has caused concern in the neighborhood. Mike Bennett is the project manager here.

Employment Conditions

- The unemployment rate in Keller is only 7.4% while the U.S. average is 8.5%. Recent job growth is positive.
- The Star Telegram reports that a Costco is being built at 8900 Tehama Ridge Pkwy which is on the west side of I-35W and just across the highway from the Alliance Town Center. The store is expected to open in late spring of 2014 and employ approximately 100 full time and 100 part time employees. The lot is reported as being 17 acres.
- Another major business that is moving near Heritage is the FAA HQ. It is reported that a new 357,214 square foot office for the FAA's southwest regional headquarters is to be built at Heritage Pkwy and I-35W on 45 acres. Construction is planned for September 2013 with an expected completion by October 2015.
- The average commute time is 34 minutes in Keller.
- The parcels on Heritage Trace Pkwy and Beach St are for retail and medical office uses only.
- In general, the Texas economy has fared better than the rest of the country through up and downturns in the economy. Typically, the annual growth rate is at least .5% higher than the national rate.
- The Fort Worth-Arlington area was ranked fifth in job creation while Dallas-Plano-Irving followed closely in sixth place.
- Since 2007 the average unemployment rate in Texas, and specifically the Dallas/Fort Worth area, has been below the national unemployment rate.
- The average hourly wage from 2010 in the Dallas/Fort Worth area is $21.89, which is just barely behind the Houston and Austin areas.

Crime Conditions

There were approximately 40 crimes reported between October 1st and October 31, 2013 in the Heritage area. 13 were theft from vehicles. 4 were assaults. 2 were thefts and 2 were burglaries.

There were approximately 30 crimes reported between November 1st and November 30, 2013 in the Heritage subdivision and surrounding areas. 10 were theft from vehicles and 16 were just thefts. Breaking and entering had 3 reports and there was 1 assault reported in the area.

Other Interesting Facts

- The Heritage subdivision is eligible for Verizon FiOS TV, internet and phone.
- In the subdivision, all of the soils are different types of clay. In our area, clay soils are one of the major factors that cause foundation problems because it contracts and expands. With an increase in moisture this causes the house to swell and making the house lift. Then it shrinks again in Texas' hot and dry summers.
  - Almost all of North Texas are sandy and clay soil. Sandy soils are the worst for foundations as they easily collapse when air pockets form causing sink holes. They are susceptible to shifting and can easily wash out. Sandy loam soil is considered the ideal soil to build a foundation on as it maintains a steady consistency/size when wet or dry.

- All of the builders in the Heritage subdivision took steps to prevent foundation damage.
- Cemetery records reveal that many of the original settlers in the Keller area were of Scots-Irish-English descent.
- DFW airport is larger than Manhattan Island.
- The term "Metroplex" was originally coined and is uniquely used to describe the Dallas/Fort Worth area. It aptly names DFW's sprawling metropolitan area that contains several cities and their suburbs.
- Texas makes 75% of the world's Snicker's bars with an M&M Mars factory located in Waco, TX.

Important Contact Information

- ❖ **HOA Contact**
  - Kyle Clawson
    - Heritagemanager@premiercommunites.net
    - (817) 741-1912
- ❖ **Heritage (Day)**
  - (817) 741-1912
- ❖ **Heritage (Emergency)**
  - (214) 871-9700
- ❖ **Electricity**
  - Tri-County Electric
    - (817) 431-1541
  - TXU Energy
    - (800) 242-9113
- ❖ **Phone, Internet and TV**
  - Verizon FiOS
    - (800) 483-4000
- ❖ **Phone**
  - One Source
    - (877) 210-3007
- ❖ **Gas**
  - Atmos Gas
    - (972) 934-9227
- ❖ **Trash/Garbage**
  - City of Fort Worth
    - (817) 392-4477
- ❖ **Water**
  - City of Ft Worth
    - (817) 392-4477
- ❖ **Sewer**
  - City of Fort Worth
    - (817) 392-4477

- ❖ **Newspaper**
  - Fort Worth Star Telegram
    - (817) 332-3333
- ❖ **Animal Control**
  - (817) 392-3737
- ❖ **Code Enforcement**
  - (817) 392-1234
- ❖ **Fire (non-emergency)**
  - (817) 922-3000
- ❖ **Police (non-emergency)**

- (817) 335-4222
- ❖ **Graffiti**
  - (817) 212-2700
- ❖ **Traffic**
  - (817) 392-2722

- ❖ **Builders**
  - D.R. Horton
    - (817) 230-0700
  - Highland Homes
    - (972) 361-9279
  - Standard Pacific Homes
    - (817) 745-0941
  - Toll Brothers Homes
    - (817) 745-0941
  - Taylor Morrison Homes
    - (281) 598-3096

- ❖ **Local Post Office**
  - Keller Post Office
    - (800) 275-8777

School Contact Information

Elementary Schools
- ❖ Bette Perot Elementary
  - (817) 744-4600
- ❖ Lone Star Elementary
  - (817) 744-5200
- ❖ Eagle Ridge Elementary
  - (817) 744-6300

Intermediate and Middle Schools
- ❖ Trinity Meadows Intermediate
  - (817) 744-4300
- ❖ Trinity Springs Middle
  - (817) 744-3500
- ❖ Parkwood Hill Intermediate
  - (817) 744-4000
- ❖ Hillwood Middle
  - (817) 744-3350
- ❖ Chisholm Trail Intermediate
  - (817) 744-3800
- ❖ Fossil Hill Middle
  - (817) 744-3050
- ❖ Timberview Middle
  - (817) 744-2600

High Schools
- ❖ Timber Creek High
  - (817) 744-2300
- ❖ Central High
  - (817) 744-2000

Sources

http://www.heritagelife.com/
http://www.bestplaces.net/city/texas/keller
http://recenter.tamu.edu/recon/main.asp?date=6/7/2013
http://www.heritagelifehoa.com
http://www.dfwrealestatematters.com/
http://www.standardpacifichomes.com/
http://www.davidweekleyhomes.com/
http://www.highlandhomes.com/
http://fortworthtexas.gov/
http://www.star-telegram.com/
https://www.crimereports.com/
http://fwbusinesspress.com/
http://websoilsurvey.nrcs.usda.gov/app/WebSoilSurvey.aspx
http://www.tshaonline.org/handbook/online/articles/hgk04
http://www.abandonedrails.com/Keller_Texas
http://foundationresolutions.com/causes-of-foundation-problems
http://ritter.tea.state.tx.us/perfreport/aeis/2011/campus.srch.html
http://www.alliancetexas.com/WhyAllianceTexas/Transportation.aspx
http://www.northtarrantexpress.com/
http://dfw.cbslocal.com/
http://texaplex.com/videos
http://www.worldpopulationstatistics.com/
http://en.wikipedia.org/wiki/

Our goal is to make a second edition of this guide.
We would love feedback, comments and suggestions for what you found helpful
and what you think could be improved in our next edition.
Please call (817) 381-3800 or email chandler@chandlercrouch.com